DENNIS STAMM

Dennis
12/12/24

Tetrahedron

A God Quad

'Love the Lord your God with all your heart and with all your soul and with all your mind and with all your strength.' The second is this: 'Love your neighbor as yourself.' There is no commandment greater than these.

Mark 12:30-31 New International Version

Contents

Acknowledgments

Thanks to my editor:
  Kathy Highfield

Prelude

O ur marriage of thirty-five years endured many challenges along the way as our years together brought much joy and contentment. Having finished raising our children and working full time jobs, life was giving the appearance that we were on the home stretch toward a happy retirement. Finding out that my wife had breast cancer introduced us to the normal steps of grief that we survived before. This time however, the word cancer seemed to impose a more devastating and traumatic level of stress, having an impact on the way I experienced the moment-by-moment events of daily life. Life has always been precious to me and this event encouraged me to place a higher priority on relationships and family. Suddenly, the contents of each day were magnified in importance, causing me to focus on every conversation and placing value on each sunrise and sunset.

While spending time with my wife in the hospital during her many surgeries and her chemotherapy treatments, memories of past life events mingled in my mind. These thoughts expressed in the following pages are a story about a great expedition that I've traveled to find the secrets of how I was created.

Perhaps one day I will be able to write down some of the complex emotional feelings that I'm experiencing as I go through this cancer with my wife, but right now I'm still sorting out my emotions a day at a time. These emotions ranged from deep depression and doubt in a pit of despair to flying high above the clouds experiencing times of wonderful loving connection with my wife and God. Just being together in a quiet room and realizing the joys we have shared over a lifetime, reflecting on each life experience that we have shared together as we recalled memories of the path we have traveled. How did all of these pieces of life chip away at this rough formless humanity to create the image that others now view when they meet me?

How is God using the events, relationships, and experiences of my lifetime to speak with me, mold me, and complete his work in me? This journal really reveals my search through a process of how I attempt to find out what life is all about and how I relate to God and others.

A Trip on a Big Pink Plane

After the troubling news of hearing my wife had breast cancer, we both felt the need to run away to a special place to think about what the news really meant to us. Having some trouble booking airplane flights and hotels, we began to wonder if we should be leaving home at this time.

Many of the details didn't seem to be sending a message of

Let's get away for a few days.

Finally, on board an airplane headed to Florida, the flight attendant came on the loudspeaker system to ask if anyone on board knew why our airplane was very special. Sitting in the front row of the airplane just inches from the flight attendant, he looked straight into my wife's eyes and said,

> *"This plane is the first in our fleet to have a pink stripe painted all around the plane because this plane is dedicated to a cure for breast cancer."*

My wife and I both broke into tears and had to later explain to the attendant why we had an outbreak of emotions. It was on this trip that I decided and felt compelled to write this journal.

I found myself reflecting back on my past and wondering why, as a child, did it trouble me so much to see my older brothers being mean to our family beagle, yet they seemed to find pleasure from doing just that. Hearing my mother and father argue, though rare, would cause me such great worry and concern. I asked myself,

> *Why was it so entertaining for some people to make fun of other people and rip them up emotionally?*

I continued asking my questions as if I was on an adventure or expedition to find answers as I treated each answer as highly valued treasures.

> *Why do many people seem to be so happy and content while other people never appear to be satisfied regardless of their circumstances?*

Growing up on a small country farm, I would often escape the ridicule of my older brothers by hiding in some secluded, isolated location. At times, I hid not only to avoid my brothers, but also I needed time to ponder on the many mysteries of life. Sometimes my hideaway was in the barn, or out in the long prairie grass by the creek behind our house, and most often I would sit in the chicken coop. I enjoyed watching and listening to the chickens interact and discovering the concept of a pecking order. There was truly a hierarchy of order in the chicken world that I observed as I watched the hens and young roosters take turns approaching the food while the dominant roosters were avoided. The pecking order took on different social orders of authority depending on the group or subgroup members. Young roosters would normally be subservient to the older roosters and they would make attempts to dominate small subgroups of hens and chicks. Occasionally these young roosters would run into a more dominant hen and would have to back down to her authority. I drew an image in my mind that my older brothers acted like these young roosters, and I concluded that my brothers knew my dad was really the head of our family pecking order. This was true unless my dad really upset my mother then I discovered,

When mamma's not happy, no one is happy.

I noted that this pecking order did have some advantages, and that the family of chickens benefited in many ways from this social system. When an owl or hawk made a screech, which is very threatening to the chickens, the roosters and hens sent out an audio warning signal and everyone hid. Likewise, if the adult chickens found a morsel of food they called out to the chicks with their unique sounding, "come and get it," and the chicks would come running.

By observing animals I learned many things about my own physical senses. But unlike my brothers, I took pity on the weak and young and sensed the pain of the one that was being picked on by the more healthy and dominating. I started to question people's motives and what inspires them to behave in a certain manner. Perhaps I was more sensitive to the weak and unhealthy because growing up I had severe eczema and psoriasis; and much of my adolescent life I had scabs and open sores all over my arms, legs, and hands. I observed that chickens and young children by nature will pick on the weak and injured when left unsupervised. I rarely experienced pity from other children and my older brothers because of my skin condition. My empathy for animals motivated me to stuff more straw into our beagle's doghouse during cold winter days or to get out of bed in the middle of the night if I forgot to feed and water the farm animals. I once angered my brothers because I freed a snake they had captured and left in a glass jar sitting in the bright sunlight. I decided I would rather face the wrath of my brothers than to bear the thought of how hot that snake would have gotten if the jar had been left in the bright sun.

At this early stage of my life it appeared to me that people are motivated by their Unconscious Physical Desires. Both of my older brothers appeared to have a desire to please their physical senses, but they also wanted to show Power and Control over the weak and meek as bullies to boost their own lack of self confidence. I took note that many people appear to spend a majority of their life indulging themselves, seeking to satisfy their physical senses, and yielding their will and decisions to what the physical senses call and yearn for.

A Few Nights in a Hotel by Mickey Mouse

S tudy and academic learning came with great difficulty in my early years of life, likely caused by a late discovery that I was nearly blind combined with my physical ailments and a serious problem with daydreaming. Finding someone to show pity and concern for this ugly duckling came from some very special people in my life. These few special heroes in my life encouraged and helped me start to blossom academically as I slowly became aware that I needed to expand my thinking processes and that I needed to study. One of my favorite quotations growing up was,

"I will study and get ready and someday my chance will come." ~Abraham Lincoln

My observations of animal and human behavior where not sufficient to fully develop my mental academic life. I began to learn from the modeling and instruction of my parents and grandparents. Even the influence of my mentors did not satisfy my thirst and appetite for knowledge.

I noted that my dad and grandfather easily outperformed me when fishing and hunting because of their experience and knowledge. Studying several books and magazine articles written by professional hunters and fisherman rapidly increased my knowledge and enhanced my abilities in these areas. It became clear to me that I would be able to advance my knowledge in other areas of life in this same manner. Reading sports magazines increased my ability to hunt and fish and therefore my skill levels were developed in academic areas using this same technique. At a young and inexperienced stage of life my physical senses continued to play a large role of persuasion and motivation. My natural human thoughts, when not controlled by a moral code of ethics, were easily manipulated by the enticement of money, pleasure, and excitement in general. These motivations spurred an early life interest in reading books about how to make large sums of money, how to enhance personal learning and memory skills, and how to be physically fit. I recognized that knowledge gave me control, not only of my ability to improve my hunting and fishing skills. but also my ability to make money. During my teen years I began to work at a large number of jobs to start saving for college, and by the time I graduated from college with my first degree I had no college debt. I started planning how to retire at a young age. My academic education combined with my physical work efforts quickly enabled me to gain Power and Control over my life circumstances.

While My Wife was Shopping for Orchids

One of these early life money making adventures occurred when a friend and I were hired to pass out sales pamphlets for one penny each. Going house to house seemed to be taking forever just to get to one hundred or one dollar. Suddenly my friend and I ran out of houses and had to cross over a very long span bridge to get to the next neighborhood. We began to think about how many steps we had to take just to make one dollar. About half way across the bridge we noticed the swift current of the river flowing far below. Suddenly my friend got this bright idea, and you guessed it, he said, "Let's throw the rest of the pamphlets into the river."

It seemed like a great idea at the time because the enticement of making lots of money without as much physical effort was mentally irresistible at this age of maturity I label the age of Ding Dong. By the time we returned to the store to collect our profits the manager had already received several phone calls complaining about the store advertising washing up on to people's lawns. Our profits quickly went down to $zero per step. The loss of profits wasn't the most important lesson learned that day.

Both my friend's mother and mine worked at the store that hired us to hand out the pamphlets. I still feel the shame and disgrace I caused my mother now, many decades later, as she looked at me with so much disappointment revealed by her expression. It was a few lessons such as this one that started to develop within my mind the relationship between the physical, mental, and social aspects of life.

One Last Night by Mickey's Place

When I was a young boy I witnessed the social order of the chickens and my older brothers; but I also observed that some of the happiest and most satisfied people, like my grandparents, had great relationships and loving connections with family, friends and neighbors. It was obvious my grandparents had a marriage that was kind and gentle, while at the same time I witnessed the failing and broken relationships of other family members that were lacking some unique element that made my grandparents relationship very special. I began to realize that to simply survive physically did not make people content but those people who developed good relationships where much happier.

I acknowledged in my own thinking that how I related to other people affected my emotional and physical well being. Even though I didn't fully understand the correlation, I knew that a hug or physical contact affected more than just my physical senses. I concluded that my physical senses had a social or community element so I began to be motivated by a Need to Adapt. These social elements were difficult to recognize and understand when I was young so I started conducting social experiments to see if I could achieve my physical needs and desires through relationships. I determined that many of the things I said or did would prevent me from getting the emotional social things I desired. Social experimentation was often painful, so mistakes in social relationship were in many ways more painful than physical testing. Watching how other people interacted became my new hobby that replaced my chicken watching days.

My very first date with a neighbor girl that I knew and occasionally walked to school with was one of these early life social experiments. A combination of not being from a very wealthy family and the fact that most eighth graders don't have much income, I took what little money I had saved over a long period of time to finance this date. We were both excited to walk across town to the County Fair, but she made it clear that she didn't want to hold hands or kiss on this date. I had recently moved from our farm in the country to the city so it was good to see the chickens at the fair. I'm not sure if my date enjoyed that part of our date as much as I did but I had a wonderful time going through the barns and watching the animals. We played a few of the sideshow games and then went on a couple of the carnival rides. Suddenly I discovered that I had run out of money and my date got very upset and said, "Is that all the money you have?"

Now, almost fifty years later I remember all of the excitement of the moment suddenly turned to embarrassment and disappointment as I still recall her exact words that day. This social experiment seemed to have gone bad, but I stored the memories to be used as a tool during later life applications.

Many of my social experiments seem to be disappointing. Slowly, through painful trials, I learned to modify my social behavior. Society chipped away at my rough edges to slowly form me into a person that was adapting to the physical, mental, and social requirements to belong to the world.

Sitting in My Wife's Doctor's Office

During adolescence I started to recognize an unknown element of life that goes beyond my human understanding. I started to ask myself,

Why was I created?
Was I an accident of nature?

I attempted to look inward for hints during my search for this unknown element of life but was unable to find the answer within. I started an exploration of the unknown, unseen world to find deeper purpose and meaning beyond the physical, mental, and social elements of life.

The First Day in Surgery

I have always had an inquisitive nature to seek out and find answers to the mysteries of the world around me. Standing in the laboratory of Thomas Edison at Greenfield Village (The Henry Ford Museum, Dearborn, Michigan), hearing the narrator tell us about how this great inventor would spend countless hours with little sleep to accomplish his goals of discovering new inventions, was very inspiring to me. Taking brief moments for a time of rest, Edison would lay down on top of his laboratory table to rest and then awaken to continue his research. People are attracted to great inventors, artists, and creative minded people because they are hoping to observe what makes them so unique. I would have loved to sit and talk to Thomas Edison or Abraham Lincoln to just watch and observe what made them so very special. What was the unique combination of factors that made them who they became? Was it their intelligence, their relationships, personality, or temperament? Were they special because of hard work and effort, a focused attention to detail, or all of these things combined with their imagination?

Thomas Edison himself was quoted as saying,

Invention is 99% perspiration and 1% inspiration.

While it is true that our time spent in perspiring may very well help us make strides toward new discoveries, there is a part of each one of us that may never make significant discovery even with great effort. Behind every great invention there is a combination of genius, vision, and imagination; but I always had to wonder if there is some other element that was not so easily discovered by observing or talking to someone. This 1% inspiration that Thomas Edison noted raised the question in my thinking,

Could this be the real spark that ignites all of the other features of our efforts and imagination?

Without inspiration all other aspects of life tend to become mundane and rather meaningless. We can spend 99% of our time reading, researching, and putting forth a tremendous effort to discover new and exciting things, but without purpose and inspiration the things we discover are somewhat meaningless.

Now a new question in my hunt for the unseen,

> *Is inspiration an external element, outside of the human ability to initiate and control?*

We search to find purpose and inspiration from many sources but what is the true source of inspiration? To realize many achievements in life, hard work is the human norm. As we have all heard it said, there are benefits to hard work and understand the warnings of slothfulness. I again asked myself where is the dividing line between our efforts in perspiration and the inspiration factor? For many years I believed that spending most of my time in study and putting forth lots of effort was surely going to, "Prepare me for my chance that will come" as my favorite Abraham Lincoln quote stated. I began to ask myself,

> *Get ready for what chance to come?*

I failed to recognize at that stage of my life that the 1% inspiration fragment was missing. With all my efforts to enhance my abilities, skills, and knowledge my efforts were rather unimportant.

Starting the First Day of Chemo

One ingredient missing or in wrong proportions can make a huge difference from a batch of cookies to a missing part in the space shuttle. When the ingredients of Inspiration & Purpose are missing many things in life fail to be truly successful. These elements are not easily found or identified because they are unlike every other part of our normal life experience. Inspiration and purpose are not something that our human senses are able to detect or recognize naturally. Our mind from early youth is accustomed to making choices primarily based on our physical senses.

The more complex a problem, the more difficult it becomes to diagnose a resolution. Purchasing an outboard boat motor manual several years ago didn't help me detect the problems I had with a boat motor. The manual I purchased was written to describe variations of motors produced over a period of several years. None of the electrical schematics, sketches, or descriptions matched my specific motor. Humans are much more complex than an outboard boat motor or even a space shuttle. The best educated, most knowledgeable medical doctors do not have a complete understanding of the human body and cancer.

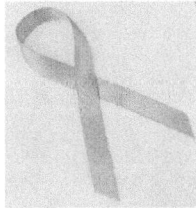

Until the middle of the eighteenth century, mankind had not even learned how to properly clean their hands prior to performing surgery, and even within the past twenty to thirty years hospital studies revealed the lack of proper hand cleaning and sterilization which continues to cause many infections and the spread of disease. Doctors prescribed bloodletting, electrical shock, and many mistreatments right up to the early part of the twentieth century. My parents recommended covering burns with butter as a cure when I was growing up. Despite us kids yelling in pain the response would always be,

A little pain a little cure.

Now we know that running cool water or an ice pack is a much better treatment for burns. Mankind's knowledge is ever changing and evolving so I had to ask a much more stirring question,

How did God create me and why?

As I stated before it is possible through observation to gain much understanding about the world, but observation alone will not reveal many of the most important complexities of mankind. This carried me to a new question,

If people avoid or ignore this unseen element of life, would this explain why humans are perplexed and confused?

I concluded that I would be required to keep an open mind to understand the world of the unseen. My family had a highly revered big dusty black book on the upper shelf in the living room. It was said to contain many answers to the world's mysteries. I wondered if the God of the universe was willing to teach and reveal answers to me if I was willing to listen and read this big black book. Could I learn about the mysteries of the unseen in this big black book?

I've shared the stories of how I began to discover the physical and social aspects of life. I've also explained the rough road I traveled during my youth in my academic life. My grandmother expressed my youth in her life journal in this fashion, "Dennis was a bit slow in school, or that was the way it seemed. They were his dreaming days." When in college I told my grandpa, "I've made up my mind that if I am ever going to learn, I will have to study."

I admired my grandparents and I believe my desire to attend church was inspired by my grandparents. Peering out of my bedroom window as a child I could see the little white country church that I attended every Sunday. The cement block base- ment had freestanding partitions that formed the classrooms where I first heard about David and the giant, Jonah and the great fish and other bible stories. My grandparents would often read me stories from a Christian children's book series. At a very early age I remember believing in Jesus and I had no reason to believe my Sunday school teachers or my grandparents would lead me down the wrong pathway.

I seldom felt comfortable taking down the big black book to read, because it was not easy for me to understand. I accepted and believed in Jesus without truly understanding what the big book had to say. I simply opened my heart and soul in faith to allow God's ray of sunshine to come in and touch me. Once I took this leap of faith I started to recognize that a change was taking place in my thought life. I had a newfound optimism that my life had great potential. This was a new confidence that my bully brothers could not easily provoke as I early started to pray for them even when they treated me poorly. I sensed that a genuine transition had taken place early in my life but I failed to gain a deep understanding of the Creator God.

A Few Days in the Hospital Again

Through my prayers I felt the need to nurture and explore my new faith into the unknown and unseen. My spirit began to develop a more joyful outreaching attitude socially toward others. I became more and more focused on others and less on myself with this new freedom within my spirit. I started to harvest love, joy, and peace as I prayed for others, caring about my friends and family as I continued on my search to find why I was born. A newfound self-confidence developed a type of freedom, which in turn made it easier to become self-indulgent.

Unfortunately, I started to believe I could function on my own without God's help, leading me down a path to seek out my natural physical desires and my need to adapt without validating the spiritual relevance of my actions. My bad habits, behavior, and attitude continued to lead me down a pathway where only empty, worthless treasures and artificial dreams could be found. I finally came to a time of final decision. Do I continue to follow my selfish desires, feed and nurture my physical social desires, or should I seek spiritual answers? I failed often to realize because of my lack of knowledge of God's instructions that my behavior was damaging my spiritual growth. I wondered if an evil force was causing me to have bad attitudes toward people with malicious attitudes as I was tempted by selfish philosophies.

You need more money!
You need more food!
You need a bigger house!
You need more things!
You need more power!
You need to be in control!
You need to have more influence!
You need to get revenge!
You need to look out for yourself!
You need to defend yourself!

When I listened and followed the goals of my selfish nature I became less concerned about the people around me. As I became more self-sufficient and selfish I started witnessing less of God's provisions and blessings. It became clear that the less concerned I became about other people, I sensed that I was drifting away from God and his blessings. I made a life choice to do whatever I could to seek after an ever-increasing closeness with the Holy Creator God of the Universe.

So my search for God continued, but where would I have to look or travel to find the secrets of the universe? I had observed chicken behavior; watched and observed people; and read many books about health, wealth, humanities, and history. I learned about great inventors, scientist, and political leaders, but I still had not found the answers to all my questions. Where should I look to find the correct pathway that leads me to the clues and secrets of the universe's perfection and the reason I was created?

Another Day in Chemo

Feared, despised, hidden, buried and burned the big black book, I again questioned if this may be where I could find the pathway that I should travel. Written by the world's most famous leaders, kings, and prophets, the Bible may very well be where I could find some answers. Stories of giants, great whales, and big large ships would possibly lead me on an adventure to find what I was looking for.

Opening the pages of this great book, I began to discover a pathway leading to someplace special that wasn't instantly obvious. Along this pathway there were clues and hints all pointing toward what I believed were the answers to my quest. When I studied and prayed with faith believing, this magical book would come alive to reveal clues to follow. Clues and hints created excitement and a sense of adventure, while I continued to move closer to an unknown prize. A strong calling was drawing me like a large magnet toward a crucial core objective that I still could not clearly distinguish.

Deceivers and make believers would often lead me off the pathway toward the promise of artificial dreams and goals as I struggled to leave my old life behind. The naysayers, the actors, the impersonators were all distracting me to achieve their own selfish purpose and objectives. Many worship the earth and the worldly created instead of the creator as they elevate themselves into roles as leaders using their wealth and influence to overtake and maintain their own small kingdoms. They offer their own wisdom as truth but quickly reveal their own egocentric ambition.

Finally getting my attitude focused on God for even a short time and disciplining my thoughts in an effort to study God's treasure map moved me forward. Doing my best to stop excluding God from my decisions and making progress so HE could reveal exciting new blessings. These times have been too infrequent when I could discipline my thinking to be less self-focused and more Godly captivated. When I surrender and continue to be faithful, I could expect to receive something very wonderful from my Father God.

My faith started to lead me down a Bible pathway that was revealing facts and clues for my success leading me toward Bible secrets. Then Bible secrets lead me to Bible treasures and then treasures in turn lead me toward Inspiration.

Finally, inspiration is where I can find my purpose and objective.

Wow, so that is where inspiration is found!

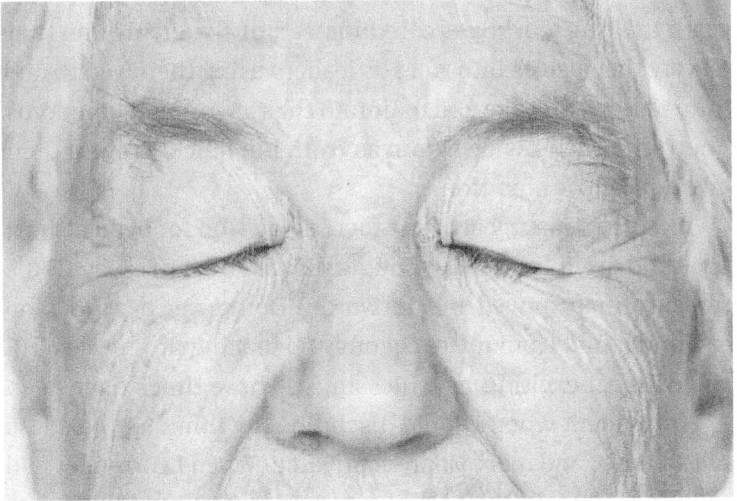

But it was to us that God revealed these things by his Spirit. For his Spirit searches out everything and shows us God's deep secrets. (I Corinthians 2:10 The New Living Translation)

One Wednesday Evening After Church

As I sat journaling in the empty church sanctuary I found myself meditating in a prayerful manner and found myself thinking about how important the Godly Inspiration element of life really is.

It is...

Essential

Mind Changing

Life Changing

Powerful

Fun

Exciting

The Key

The Peace

The Fruit

The Joy

The Mystery

Finally, I determined that the 1% factor of Inspiration is where I begin to find my purpose.

Home Alone When My Wife is in the Hospital

As my wife lay in the hospital, I remembered a time long ago when I came to a point of impasse in my thinking. I envisioned my life search coming to the edge of a cliff that had a long high bridge over a deep valley and river.

This bridge that I was afraid to cross represented my feeling of doubt if I was truly worthy of God's love. I asked myself,

Am I really valuable to God and deserving of the love of an everlasting, unlimited, most holy, powerful, Creator God?

In my weakest moments when I realized that I have a sinful, wicked, hateful, revengeful, and immature nature, I speculated if I deserved the love of a mighty God. This was truly a sad time indeed when I came to understand, when standing peering over to the other side of this deep valley between me and God, that I am not deserving and can never become worthy of God's love. Even if I do my very best and maintain a great attitude for short periods of time, I still fall so very short of being who God wants me to be. Right at that moment I found myself defeated and depressed and in such a deep need. I felt I had come to the end of my exciting expedition searching for answers in the Bible.

After a serious time of prayer and meditation I envisioned someone walking toward me from the other side of this bridge that crossed the deep valley. An overwhelming sense of anxious anticipation started to grow inside of me as this person came closer and closer to me. I sensed something exciting was about to happen. Suddenly in my depressed dream of slumber I recognized that it was Jesus standing there before me on the bridge with an outstretched hand as he spoke to me,

> *My grace is sufficient to cover all your sin ... now come with me to a wonderful land beyond where all your questions will be answered.*

My emotions and thoughts instantly became more positive that wonderful night as I lay in my bed praying, finally realizing that because of Jesus' sacrifice I was made worthy to cross this bridge with Jesus beside me. I once again started my exciting expedition by reading the promises of God in the big black book. I knew at that very moment that I wanted to make a commitment to trust God and that my life would never be the same.

My life made a transition that night as I entered a place that was magical, where vision and imagination became possible, a land filled with encouragement found in trust and faith in the unseen. My perception of the world became strangely dim as God started to create for me a clearer vision of the concealed. I started to acknowledge that God has always performed wonders and once I surrendered my will in obedience I started to witness more and more miracles and treasures. I suddenly began to understand that I had missed opportunities and blessings because I had not yielded my willingness to God, and I sought to change my behavior to avoid any further loss of blessings. I started to appreciate that God's miracles are not what the world thinks of as miracles. God's miracles are more satisfying, more significant than what the unbelieving person could conceive of or at times even understand or comprehend. Marriages are healed, relationships grow, and motivation and purpose are fresh and new. Suddenly I thought back to the life of my grandparents and now I understood this was the secret to their happiness, joy, and peace.

Home with My Wife After a Hospital Stay

I now realized that I was starting to get it, but recognized I had a long journey ahead of me. Each time I discovered a clue to my many questions each answer would bring about new questions to seek out yet another answer. As I followed each Bible clue and secret it would lead me to a new problem to resolve in my understanding. I was slowly making a transition from my natural human understanding of the world toward a better perception of the world as God viewed each person's life plan.

Research, education of any kind, begins with key questions. As my quest for information and knowledge continued, I determined that I must ask the correct questions to get the answers I was seeking. My early life observations taught me many things about the physical world, followed by my academic life where I learned the three Rs. Socially my life lessons will continue for a lifetime, but it wasn't until after I crossed that high bridge of faith and trust that I found inspiration hidden in the Bible. Each answer that I searched for with a proper attitude and motive would move God to a willingness to reveal new exciting concepts to me. God is only willing to reveal his truth in a time that fits into his plan and purpose for my life.

This brings me to a point of explaining some wonderful inspiring things that God has revealed to me as I searched the Bible treasure land over the past several years.

Several early 20th century philosophers and psychologists developed their theories regarding personality and human behavior. Carl G. Jung was puzzled in the 1920s by several of the theoretical concepts of his mentor, Sigmund Freud. While Freud was certain that humans are motivated by Unconscious Physical Desires (Freud, 1923), as far as Jung was concerned, people are motivated by the Need to Adapt (Jung, 1921). Jung believed that the human search for pleasure (physical desire) is only one of our adaptational strategies as humans. A few years later, Alfred Adler developed yet another theory of personality behavior proclaiming that the basic human motive is based on our need to establish Power and Control (Adler, 1964).

Jung eventually thought that human personality encompassed all of these things: the need for pleasure and relationship, the drive for power and control, and the motivation to adapt. Because each of these different men, Freud, Adler, and Jung had each created a psychological theory that was different, this led Jung to believe each person develops an individual sense of reality according to our own Psychological Type. Jung began to construct what he believed was a unifying (Combined) theory that would allow each view its own integrity.

Jung explored many different theories of personality that were devised throughout history. Jung was surprised during his research by the fact that many of the theories describing human character in terms of four basic classifications. One of the oldest was Astrology, which classifies human character in terms of the four elements: water, air, earth, and fire. Greek Medicine classified people in terms of bodily secretions, which gave us our four words: phlegmatic, sanguine, choleric, and melancholic.

The Tarot Cards relate personalities to the four suits of cards: wands, cups, swords, and pentacles. These where converted later to our current modern card suits of clubs, hearts, spades, and diamonds. Jung realized that the four categories in each of these schemes, in his opinion, were fairly consistent, and he believed this represented four basic ways humans perceive or understand reality. Jung believed his own original theory and concepts of human behavior, as well as that of Freud and Adler, had emphasized only one of the four which corresponded to his own way of approaching reality.

Ultimately, Jung concluded that we are all born with four psychological functions: Sensation, Intuition, Thinking, and Feeling (Jung, 1971). This eventually developed into the Myers Briggs (MB) personality profiling theory (Briggs, 1987). This theory includes the concept of how Four Pairs of different personality types approach and perceive reality. The MB personality type test determines individual's normal or preferred fashion of dealing with reality and is essentially a combination of theoretical philosophies. Freud analyzed personality in terms of feelings, the human need to relate to our environment, while Alfred Adler emphasized people's motives as thinking, the ability to predict and control our circumstances.

I'll continue to explain my findings about these men later, but let me first explain my process of finding Biblical truth. I now started to ask compelling questions that would require me to search the Bible to find answers to much more challenging topics.

Back to Finish Up Chemo

My quest for knowledge of human behavior started way back when I watched the chickens and progressed to the observation and interaction of family members to learn how society was organized. Before studying the Bible and psychologists' viewpoints, before I started my parenting responsibilities or church leadership roles, I believed that the Creator God had all the answers to my questions. My quest and adventure took me on a wonderful journey to search and find what motivates and inspires humanity and what really makes us tick. From my study of the Bible I discovered that our lives contain several different elements that make up who we are. One of the first places I noticed some of these elements was in the first commandment,

Love the Lord your God with all your Heart, Soul, Mind,
and Strength. (see Deuteronomy 10:12)

Years later in my studies I discovered that Jesus, when being questioned about what was the most important commandment, Jesus quoted this same verse, only he added to this verse and revealed another human element.

Love the Lord your God with all your Heart, Soul, Mind, and Strength, and Love your Neighbor as yourself. (see Mark 12:30–31)

Another Chemo Session

At this early stage of my search it appeared there might be three, four, or even five elements that make up who we are according to many of the Old and New Testament scriptures. I asked a series of other questions to help me search for what God wanted to reveal to me.

What is the Heart and Soul that scripture is talking about?

Now I had a good idea what the mind was referencing but I still asked myself,

Does love the Lord your God with your mind mean mankind's brain, or thinking?

I also asked other questions.

Does love the Lord your God with your strength mean mankind's physical body and strength?
How do I love God with my strength?

Then finally I asked myself,

Why did Jesus include this last part in his answer to their question – Love your neighbor as yourself?

Many years prior to even starting this Bible study for answers I attended a Sunday school class which was led by a previous pastor's wife using as a textbook, *The Pursuit of Holiness* by Jerry Bridges (1978).

More recently, I referenced this book in preparation of an adult Sunday school lesson I was going to teach. I found an excellent definition of Heart and Soul in this book and I quote out of the book what I believe was the answer to my first question above, "What is the Heart and Soul?"

I quote from the book as follows,

> *Heart in Scripture is used in various ways. Sometimes it means our reason or understanding, sometimes our affections and emotions, and sometimes our will. Generally it denotes the whole soul of man and all its faculties, not individually, but as they all work together in doing good or evil. The mind as it reasons, discerns, and judges. The emotions as they like or dislike; the conscience as it determines and warn; and the will as it chooses or refuses – are all together called the heart. (Bridges, 1978)*

I pursued each of my questions as I continued to study when my busy schedule allowed, discovering many scriptures that addressed my questions. Each time God revealed a new part of this puzzle I got excited and thirsted for more answers. The Bible's clear message to love the Lord our God is always the top priority of God. We are to love God above everything else, placing the spiritual part of our life as our top priority.

It became clear in Matthew chapter five, that the spiritual takes priority over the physical (body) part of our life.

If your right eye causes you to sin, gouge it out and throw it away. It is better for you to lose one part of your body than for your whole body to be thrown into hell. And if your right hand causes you to sin, cut it off and throw it away. It is better for you to lose one part of your body than for your whole body to go into hell. (Matthew 5:29-30 New International Version)

When I read the Apostle Paul's letter to the Romans chapter eight, it states that we have a choice of what to fill our minds with. The question of loving the Lord with our entire mind seems to be partially answered by this scripture.

Those who live according to the sinful nature have their minds set on what that nature desires; but those who live in accordance with the Spirit have their minds set on what the Spirit desires. The mind of the sinful man is death, but the mind controlled by the Spirit is life and peace; the sinful mind is hostile to God. It does not submit to God's law, nor can it do so. (See Romans 8:5-7)

Back in the Hospital

A ccording to much of the Apostle Paul's writing, we have a choice of what to fill our minds with. What we watch, listen to, and as our surroundings and circumstances complete a puzzle of how we ultimately make decisions. The Bible is full of verses that identify those things that I should fill my mind with. This next verse identifies the physical as our body and indicates the priority of the academic (mental) and spiritual over the physical. I Timothy chapter 4 states,

> *Have nothing to do with godless myths and old wives'*
> *tales; rather, train yourself to be godly. For physical*
> *training is of some value, but godliness has value for*

all things, holding promise for both the present life and the life to come. (I Timothy 4: 7-8 New International Version)

As I continued to isolate the separate parts of how we were constructed, there also appeared to be a priority of order between the parts of humanity. Several verses in the Bible indicate the social portion of the life elements have priority over the mental and physical. There are scriptures that tell us that the way we show our love for God is revealed or shown by the way we treat others. Jesus said,

As you treat each of these (Children) you show how you also love me. (See Matthew 25:40)

The book of Matthew chapter five goes so far as to say the following,

Therefore, if you are offering your gift at the altar and there remember that your brother has something against you, leave your gift there in front of the altar. First go and be reconciled to your brother; then come and offer your gift. (Matthew 5:23-24 New International Version)

This verse not only indicates a very high priority on the social / relational but it also fills the requirement to place God first because God has commanded us to love each other.

The more I studied scripture I started forming an image of what God's priorities in life should be. I know Christ is that perfect image of what God desires as an example for mankind, and I was attempting to see the individual parts to gain a better insight of how we are put together. By this time in my studies it appeared that God had shown me four separate parts or elements of our makeup as humans which brought me back to Mark chapter twelve.

> *Love the Lord your God with all your heart and with all your soul (Spiritual) and with all your mind (Mental) and with all your strength. (Physical) The second is this: 'Love your neighbor as yourself. (Social) (Mark 12:30-31 New International Version)*

I believe the Bible not only establishes the make up of mankind but that it also tells us the priority of each fundamental part of our make up as human beings. (In my Parenting book titled: *Grape Jelly*, I label these parts as Growth Groups).

By reading and studying God's word, we gain a better understanding of the Creator God as well as a better understanding of ourselves. Throughout the Bible, God indicates how he made or designed mankind and how we should prioritize the different aspects of our lives. Searching scriptures with a correct attitude and spirit reveals exciting things about the true nature of mankind. I came to believe that mankind can learn much from observing God's creation in nature and the world around us, but mankind too is a created being. We can never truly discover the Creator God or the true nature of the world without God's indwelling Holy Spirit (The inspiration Factor).

Nearly Complete with Chemo

After years of working in management, I've been required to attend a number of educational courses regarding personality profile testing and temperament testing. When my management position required me to study industrial psychology and personality profiling I began to notice some similarities between my Bible studies about mankind's makeup and the work materials that I was required to study. I noted that most of these tests are fairly good at determining some of the characteristics of different personality types. During the last several years while researching the subject of this journal I found that most of the tests fall short of identifying people's true nature. I believe the missing ingredient that is lacking is an understanding of the spiritual nature of mankind.

Prior to a person's Christian conversion, these secular personality tests appear to be more accurate because people are fundamentally operating without God's Holy Spirit influence. Freud, Alder, and Jung excluded the spiritual from their analysis, so without the influence of the spiritual, a person is likely to respond and react in a manner that is human but not necessarily Christ-like. Again as Paul said in his letter to the Romans,

Those who live according to the sinful nature have their minds set on what that nature desires. (See Romans 8:5)

This statement certainly describes the Freudian perception that mankind is motivated by Unconscious Physical Desires. Likewise this verse describes the Adler perception that mankind is motivated by Power and Control.

Our physical bodies are very much a part of who we are but our physical senses YELL out and make demands, but Christ followers must shadow Paul's example doing our best to make our body a slave to our spirit. Paul's letter of First Corinthians, chapter nine states the following.

> Everyone who competes in the games goes into strict training. They do it to get a crown that will not last; but we do it to get a crown that will last forever. Therefore I do not run like a man running aimlessly; I do not fight like a man beating the air. No, I beat my body and make it my slave so that after I have preached to others, I myself will not be disqualified for the prize. (I Corinthians 9:25-27 New International Version)

Paul wrote to the Galatians in chapter two of that book of the bible,

> I have been crucified with Christ; and it is no longer I who live, but Christ lives in me; and the life which I now live in the flesh I live by faith in the Son of God, who loved me and gave Himself up for me. (Galatians 2:20 New International Version)

Jesus shows how he valued even our physical well being when he healed illnesses and gave a drink of water to the woman at the well. James says that if we don't meet the physical needs of others our faith is dead. James writes in chapter two of that book,

> Suppose a brother or sister is without clothes and daily food. If one of you says to him, Go, I wish you well; keep warm and well fed, but does nothing about his physical needs, what good is it. In the same way faith by itself if

not accompanied by action, is dead. See (James 2:15-17)

Wife at Home in Recovery

Now I will head back to psychologist Jung's theories to determine how his research compares to my Bible research regarding human behavior. Jung's four psychological functions: Sensation, Intuition, Thinking, and Feeling from a worldly (non-Christian) perspective are fairly close to the separate functions I discovered in the scriptures, Physical, Spiritual, Mental, and Social (Jung, 1971).

The MB four pairs also come close to these separate functions I found as I clarify as follows.

- M/B 1st Pair: Extraversion / Introversion (Energy), roughly correlates with the Physical
- M/B 2nd Pair: Sensing / Intuition (Information), roughly correlates with the Mental
- M/B 3rd Pair: Thinking / Feeling (Decisions), roughly correlates with the Spiritual
- M/B 4th Pair: Judging / Perceiving (Lifestyle), roughly correlates with the Social

The primary difference between the biblical and worldly concepts being, the priority and focus on self verses a focus on the Creator God and other people. Christ followers view the physical world as temporal, their minds understand information differently, decisions are made from a spiritual perspective, and their social lifestyles highly value relationships.

A Memory of Past Events

Many years ago, even prior to starting my search for the separate functions of mankind and prior to my work management years, my wife and I made a very difficult decision as to how we wanted to educate our children. After much prayer and discussion we chose to send our children to a private elementary Christian School. Recently, as I was digging through some of my old files preparing to teach a Children's Sunday school lesson, I found our kids Christian school motto. The school motto was

God / Parents / Church / School

That partnership and priority appeared at that time we enrolled our children to be very biblical and correct. These four elements seemed to be the correct combination of essentials to raise godly, Christian children especially in the world we live in today. These priorities also correlate with the four life elements I had found in the twelfth chapter of the book of Mark.

In recent years I enrolled in a management course that studied how to mentor people in the work place. This particular course stated that there are four fundamental steps in the process of mentoring or training people. The number four was mysteriously recurring in several of the different materials I had been studying. I also remembered that Professor Jung had witnessed a similar pattern of reoccurring fours during his studies.

The four learning steps of training people in the workplace are as follows.

- Step 1: Directive – show and tell (Informational)
- Step 2: Coaching – close physical oversight
- Step 3: Encouraging – occasional support
- Step 4: Delegate / Advice – resourcing experience

It wasn't until I was taking a class in ministry that I finally received a major clue to my twenty year search. I received insight during one particular class assignment, which was to study and prepare a comparative analysis of the four gospels.

Over a period of a few weeks I studied each of the four gospels carefully and developed a short summary of the main content of each of these first four books of the New Testament. The professor suggested that as students we should begin our study by asking ourselves these questions.

- *Why four Gospels?*
- *Why are they all slightly different?*
- *What is God attempting to show us or tell us?*

•

Study Results from My Classes in Ministry

A summary of my class notes from the four gospels looked something like this.

The Gospel of Matthew

The Gospel of Matthew contains evidence and historical proof of the Messiahship of Christ including the following.

- Old Testament references linking the old and new testaments
- Christ's family history / linage
- Reference to Jesus as Son of David
- Explanation of Christ fulfillment of Old Testament prophesies
- Christ referenced as the Son of Abraham

The facts of

- His background (genealogy)
- His birth
- His announcement of birth

- His place of birth
- His adoration as a baby
- His baptism
- His temptations
- His Inauguration as King
- His admission that he is the Messiah

The Gospel of Mark

The Gospel of Mark contains evidence and revealed Christ's humanity and his servitude including the following.

Christ as a Servant

- His human suffering
- His temptation as a man
- His sacrifice for others
- His service to others
- His example (and illustrations)
- His healing and concern for human frailties and the human condition
- His call of the 12 and his friendship with them
- His parable reflections of his understanding of the human condition
- His attitudes of thoughtfulness about sickness and death
- His feeding of food to the thousands of hungry
- His looking out for people being taken advantage of in the temple by the money changers
- His humility riding a donkey colt

The Gospel of Luke

The Gospel of Luke reveals Jesus attitude toward others including the following.

- The story of the Good Samaritan.

The uncommon interest in individuals like

- Zaccheus
- The penitent thief
- The Story of the Prodigal Son
- The Penitent publican
- The Lepers
- His constant prayer for others
- The prominent place he gave to women, which wasn't the cultural norm
- His sacrificial giving attitude toward those in poverty
- Called (The Son of Man) – describing his humanity
- Ministries to the sick, sinful, physically needy, and the socially unpopular...
- His love for the paralytic, the diseased, people with deformities, also his attitudes and thoughts toward government, church leaders, greed, covetousness, hypocrisy, and forgiveness

The Gospel of John

The Gospel of John – John's approach is the most Theological of the four gospels where Christ is declared the following.

STUDY RESULTS FROM MY CLASSES IN MINISTRY

Christ the Divine Son of God.

Titles used by John for Jesus

The Word was God

- The Divine
- The Lamb of God
- The Holy Sacrifice
- The Messiah
- The Son of God
- The King of Israel
- The Savior of the World
- The Lord and God

Jesus' deity also asserted in a series of I Am claims and other I Am statements Christ made implicit and explicit claim to be the I AM, Yahweh of the Old Testament.

Jesus – 7 signs / miracles were told in the Gospel of John 11: 25-26.

One Inspired Evening as My Wife was Recovering

T hen one night as I started to cry with joy, God revealed and confirmed that which I had been looking for over many years. An unexplained exhilaration came over me that was beyond simply thinking,

I get it!

Now, fully believing that after all my years of searching, I was receiving a message from the Creator God. Wow...what a wonderful feeling that the Creator God was revealing a prize to me after years of following the Bible clues and secrets. An inspirational moment of discovery that my hard work (Perspiration) and efforts could never have accomplished.

An epiphany!

God's message that came to me that evening was not in an audible voice or anything like that but my very Heart of Hearts sensed that God had revealed this special treasure of discovery as if I had found a pearl of great value. I ask myself,

Have others felt the very presence of God when they discovered Bible treasures?

That special night God's Spirit and the Bible treasure map lead me to understand and revealed the

Tetrahedron
A God Quad

The Gospel of Matthew represents the factual evidence including Christ family linage and explains intellectually, God's plan to bring about the divine birth of Jesus, which corresponds to the Mental part of our make up.

Lord, I love you with my Mind.

The Gospel of Mark explains Christ's humanity by describing his servitude and suffering, illuminating the fact that Jesus was all God and all Man. This book correlates to the Physical part of our make up.

Lord I love you with all my Strength.

The Gospel of Luke illustrates Christ's loving attitude toward others like the poor, the sinners, lowly, and the downtrodden. This book correlates to the Social or relational.

Lord I will love you by loving others.

The Gospel of John describes Christ as the Son of God, the Mighty God, our Savior and Redeemer. Lord you are the Sacrificial Lamb the Messiah who loves me unconditionally. This gospel corresponds to the Spiritual.

Lord I love you with all my Heart and Soul.

Back in the Hospital Again

N ow many things in the past begin to make sense.

The Christian School motto had four team members

God – The Spiritual

- The Holy Spirit's enlightenment

Parents – The Physical

- Training / exampling behavior

Church – The Social

- Relationship, attitude, humility

School – The Mental

- Academic, information

The four steps of mentoring and teaching others

Show and tell direction

- The Mental – teaching and information

Coaching – The Physical

- Parenting, close oversight

Encouragement – The Social

- The church / family

Delegate / Advice

- The Spiritual – Resources of decision-making

The four Gospels

Matthew

- The Mental - factual evidence of Jesus family lineage

Mark

- The Physical - Christ's humanity

Luke

- The Social - Christian attitudes toward others

John

- The Spiritual – Jesus is the High Priest and our spiritual resource.

The Tetrahedron a God Quad

The four elements of how we are made and put together, listed in the priority revealed in Scriptures.

1. The Spiritual
2. The Social
3. The Mental
4. The Physical

Describing that sense, feeling, and knowledge that God has communicated with me along this long search for Bible secrets has left me

INSPIRED.

Each Bible clue, secret and treasure on my path of discovery kept me excited and motivated. When I learn to listen and study without selfish motive I continue to find just how wonderful the Big Black Book has became as a life resource.

A Late Night of Study and Meditation

I t is difficult for me to describe those wonderful, exciting times, those highly sensitive rare occasions when my attitude is correct, my attention is focused, my spirit is open and surrendered, when God speaks and I am listening. I discover confidence, peace, conviction, joy, hope, and reassurance. I find myself feeling empowered, submissive, modest, and wanting to worship God. I gain a desire to praise God, no longer feeling the need to get revenge, no longer needing to be in control, and no longer needing to always worry.

Although these times have been less often then I would have liked, I know there could have been more opportunities for God to speak with me if I listened and prayed more often.

Often those times when God has talked to me were times when major decisions were required of me or when my life was in chaos and I had to just stop to listen to God. Maybe someday I will more readily ask for God's help and be quicker to surrender to his will and desire for my life. God has a deep desire to be involved in every detail of our lives and sent his one and only Son to show us his love.

A Time of Reflection on a Cruise Ship

With this new revolutionary treasure, my view became much clearer as I stood looking back to reflect on what I had misinterpreted in the past. My new mindset with spiritual spectacles would now reveal how blind I was before and how my vision had improved. I began to ask new questions and continued down a new pathway as I entered into a land of enchantment. Along this new path of trust and faith, things around me began to sparkle and glisten like a snowflake in the bright sunlight. People appeared to have more potential, as the world previously appeared dingy and dull, I could now better visualize God's wonderful plan for my life and the lives of others.

I ask a new question,

> *How do people's personalities change or become enhanced when they accept Christ as their personal savior?*

I've attempted to answer this new question by looking at how each of the Myers Briggs four psychological functions of: Sensation, Intuition, Thinking, and Feeling could change when becoming a Christ follower. I've broken down the four pairs developed by the MB personality profiling theory and analyzed them separately.

I've given each of the MB four pairs a new title that I believe may better describe the way a Christian may live and respond to people around them after they have decided to follow Christ. The MB personality profiling, as stated earlier, tests an individual's preferred fashion of dealing with life by grouping people's personality preferences into four pairs or eight different mannerisms or ways of making life choices.

In each of the following examples, in addition to the significance of the name I've given to the four pairs. I've also shown a Before and After section in my analogy. The Before and After will hopefully better explain the transformation that occurs in a person's life after their choice to become a disciple of Christ.

MB FOUR PAIRS (Briggs, 1987)

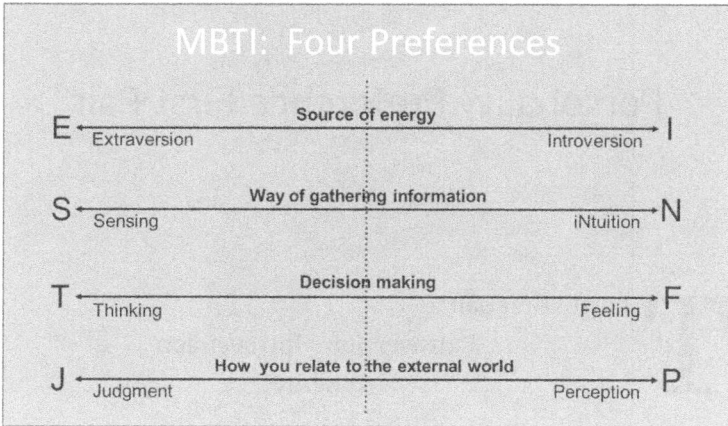

MBTI: Four Preferences

E	Source of energy	I
Extraversion		Introversion
S	Way of gathering information	N
Sensing		iNtuition
T	Decision making	F
Thinking		Feeling
J	How you relate to the external world	P
Judgment		Perception

Compared with the

GOD QUAD

1. Spiritual. 2. Social 3. Mental. 4. Physical

Personality Preference First Pair

T he MB first pair...
>   Extraversion / Introversion
>   (Energy)

My first GQ (God Quad) pair title is...
>   Engaged / Mentoring–Advisor
>   (Physical)

Transformation explanation

Extraversion vs. Engaged

MB   GQ

(Myers Briggs) (God Quad)

MB asks the following question about the Extraversion personality preference.

> *Do you prefer to focus on the outer world or on your own inner world?*

An Extraversion type personality, per MB, gets energy from an active involvement in situations and from being around other people. They are comfortable in groups, are outgoing, and can better understand a problem if they can talk out loud about it or when hearing others discuss an issue.

Christ followers that had been 'Extraverted' personalities may change in the following manner once they become faithful believers. Their personal mannerism may transform into a GQ Engaged' personality type resulting in a more Christ like relationship with other people.

GQ Engaged

This Engaged type of person begins to understand that other people need them to step up and take an active involved role in a situation because of their experience and understanding. They recognize the situation can be improved or the attitudes of those involved can be steered in a more Godly positive direction with their engagement.

Before & After their Christian transformation experience

Before this person became a Christian, they were often Extraverted for their own glory and recognition or to seek popularity. Before becoming a Christian they had a difficult time knowing their God created purpose but were focused on their own purpose and objectives.

After becoming a Christian they became more Engaged and interested in the welfare of other people, leading them to a better understanding of people, which converts acquaintances into friendships. This transition in turn helps them realize that they need relationships to be truly successful as opposed to needing others to boost their own self-image or to be recognized by others. Suddenly they become more outreaching, more caring;

leading them into highly valued relationships.

Transitioning from Extraverted to becoming more Engaged, this person starts to witness that they are no longer as motivated by self-interest; realizing that to respect and build up others is very rewarding. After accepting Christ and reading God's Word this person starts to understand Bible secrets, which points toward a life purpose and plan, teaching them to search for God's purpose in every situation.

<u>Introversion vs. Mentoring-Advisor</u>
MB   GQ

MB asks again the following question.

Do you prefer to focus on the outer world or on your own inner world?

An Introversion type personality per MB gets energy from dealing with ideas, pictures, memories, and reactions that are inside their head, in their inner world. This introversion personality prefers to do things alone or with a few limited number of people, likes ideas, and normally gives the appearance of someone that is reflective or reserved.

Christ followers that have been Introverted personalities in the past may change once they become faithful believers. The GQ Mentoring / Adviser type personality may transform their personal preferences in the following manner.

GQ Mentoring / Adviser
As a Christ follower this person may suddenly realize circum-

stances require them to spend more of their time observing and thinking about how they can support a situation and by helping those who are engaged in leading an effort. This person works well when they sit back and observe an activity or situation and help in a more quiet and thoughtful (less engaged) manner. This person enjoys researching concepts and spending much time thinking about what motivates people.

Before & After their Christian transformation experience

Before their Christian transformation this Introverted person's thoughts were self-focused, spending much of their time sheltering and protecting themselves from being harmed by others. After their decision to follow Christ, they transformed their attitudes from Introverted to Mentoring-Advisor. People around them begin to recognize that they want to be more helpful. This not only improves their self-evaluation but also converts friendships into long-term relationships. Suddenly these changes in this person's motives transform their world from a small internal world that contained only selfish dreams and purpose into a new exciting land of adventure. Finally coming to understand that God is in control and protecting them, they begin to learn to enjoy life and start becoming more excited about being a part of God's wonderful plan for their life and help lead others to find their purpose in life. God's plan begins to appear piece by piece as this person learns to trust and obey God, while they work to improve their love toward others.

Personality Preference Second Pair

The MB second pair is...
                    Sensing–Intuition
                    (Information)

My second GQ title...
                    Sensory–Scrutinizing
                    (Mental)

MB with regards to these two preferences asks these two questions.

> *Do you prefer to focus on the basic information you take in or do you prefer to interpret and add meaning?*

> *Do you pay more attention to information that comes in through your senses (Sensing), or do you pay more attention to the patterns and possibilities that you see within the information you receive (Intuition)?*

MB says everyone spends some time Sensing and some time using Intuition but states to not confuse the MB term Sensing with sensual (or sensitive), as they define these terms they are not related. Sensing people tend to pay attention to physical reality: what they see, hear, touch, taste, and smell.

Sensing vs. Sensory

MB   GQ

The MB definition of a Sensing person is concerned with what is actual, present, current, and real. They notice facts and remember details that are important to them. They see the practical side of things and learn best from experience. Christ Followers that have been Sensing personalities types may change once they become faithful believers. This GQ Sensory type personality may convert to the following changes in personality preference as they begin to live a Christian life.

GQ Sensory

As a Christ follower this person has an understanding of relations based largely on or affected by their physical senses and by the physical response they receive when interacting with other people. This person observes the way people respond and react to situations believing this exhibits their passions thus revealing what they value. This Sensory personality type of person makes decisions based on their life observation of people, which helps guide their choices and decisions. Using their Sensory characteristics, this person attempts to evaluate people's priorities.

Before & After their Christian transformation experience

Prior to this person's Christian transformation they would spend much time observing (Sensing) people's reactions but often with self-serving or lustful intentions. Sensing people's physical reactions gave them a strategic advantage when competing against others for authority, popularity, or physical gratification. Before their Christian conversion, this person lived cautiously because of the realization that their own actions/reactions send a message to other people about what is valued, exposing selfish intentions. This would then in turn lead toward deceptive cover ups and attempts to live their life misleading others.

After accepting Christ this person becomes less self-focused and more outwardly focused on others. This personality's Sensing type character begins to be converted from an animalist type of self-preservation into a Sensory type of relational attribute, which is utilized to build stronger relationships. This converted new Sensory personality type begins to start looking beyond people's initial reactions, attempting to better understand why people react and respond as they do, enabling them to build better relationships. Discovering that people normally respond in a manner that is self-protective, and now as a Christ follower they become more relational with people and by using carefully chosen words it helps this Sensory person build better friendships.

Intuition vs Scrutinizing

MB   GQ

The MB Intuition type personality is concerned with impressions or the meaning and patterns of information they receive. This MB type would rather learn by thinking through a problem than by living a hands-on experience and often thinks about the future more than the past. This MB type remembers events more as an impression of what it was like than the actual facts or details of what occurred.

Christ followers that have been Intuitive personalities in the past may change once they become faithful believers. The GQ Scrutinizing type personality may adapt to the following changes in personality preference after they decide to be Christians.

GQ Scrutinizing

This person studies people's response in different situations and attempts to see what their goals and objectives are as related to differing circumstance. They attempt to understand the long-term effects of their own or others behavior in relationships. Sometimes they may seem a little out of touch with people's feelings because they don't pay as much attention to the small details in a conversation as much as they attempt to analyze a person's overall intentions.

Before & After their Christian transformation experience

Before this person's conversion they would tend to analyze people's motives and actions to better prepare themself for their own defense or for self-advancement. They would often use their ability to understand others for selfish gain or to manipulate situations. After their Christian transformation this person learned to overlook an offense or to look beyond a person's surface actions and reactions. They learn the unnatural or Christ-like manner to respond to situations and became cautious about how they respond to any given situation. They often will develop a strategic plan to seek wise counsel from a good Christian friend or pastor before making important decisions.

Personality Preference Third Pair

T he MB third pair is...
Thinking / Feeling
(Decisions)

The GQ new titles for these two preferences are...
Meditative / Compassionate
(Spiritual)

This area of personality is complex and plays a major role in our decision-making as well as the forth pair of personality preferences discussed next. Often the type of decision being made and the people involved can affect what we ultimately decide in any given situation. This area of our personality preference is most closely identified with our Heart & Soul or the Spiritual part of our life. Naturally, all of the events and people in our lives play an important role in our decision-making. Certainly our physical reality and mental database (experiences) of previous situations also contribute to our decision-making. This area of life and personality has been influenced by all experiences over a lifetime. All of the experiences of life including things seen, heard, and touched, have influenced a person's development and who they have become.

MB asks two questions when making decisions.

Does this personality type prefer to first look at logic and consistency or first look at the people and the special circumstances involved?

Does the person like to put more weight on objective principles and impersonal facts (Thinking) or do they put more weight on personal concerns and the people involved (Feeling)?

MB makes the distinction to clarify that Feeling, as they define it in this personality type, should not be confused with emotion and that Thinking should not be confused with intelligence. MB states that everyone uses Thinking for some decisions and Feelings for other decisions or that both may be used to weigh a decision.

Thinking vs Meditative
MB   .   GQ

The MB Thinking type personality is concerned with logic and the facts. Truth is often favored over tact for this personality type and decisions weigh pros and cons in a given situation. I describe the GQ Meditative personality as follows. Christ Followers that have been Thinking personalities may change once they become faithful believers into a GQ Meditative type personality and witness the following revised or new personality preferences.

GQ Meditative

This person now attempts to apply Biblical principles and concepts that may or may not be culturally popular. This mindful thought process can be overly analytical if taken to an extreme and may often lack compassion so the Meditative thought process should be weighted against a Christ like attitude of compassion and love for others.

Before & After their Christian transformation experience

Before this person changed they would look (Think) how the outcome of a situation would affect them. Their decision-making would analyze situations hoping to be self-promoting or to justify their own choices. The facts of information obtained through analysis would help them build a case of pros and cons to formulate a choice that was personally most beneficial.

After they become a Christ follower this person will look to God's Word or ask good example Christian advisors to help figure out their options. Before this person accepted Christ they would often believe that Truth or Facts were the most important factor in a decision even if bringing out truth harmed others. After accepting Christ they are still concerned about truth but they begin to understand that even God is careful when and where to reveal His Truth to people. Finally realizing that there may be a better time and place to share information with others when they are ready and prepared to receive it. In their new Christian pathway the Meditative personality discovers that a time of prayer may help prepare them to face any given situation and to make wiser life choices.

Feeling vs Compassionate
MB   GQ

The MB Feeling type personality is largely based on making decisions by weighing what people care about and their point of view. The MB Feeling personality type is concerned with values and what is the best for the people involved, and because of this they often make decisions to maintain harmony and may have caring relationships. I describe the GQ Compassionate personality as follows. Christ Followers that have been Feeling personalities may change once they become faithful believers. The GQ Compassionate type personality may transform in the following manner.

GQ Compassionate

Being generous and caring for the needs of others, sometimes they find that they act in a reactionary fashion and don't spend enough time meditating about the long-term outcome of their actions. It is biblical to be compassionate but sometimes this person tends to over obligate him or herself.

Before & After the Christian transformation experience

Before this type of person found and followed Christ, their own popularity played a large roll when making decisions as well as effecting their generosity to others. This person discovers that sometimes they were enabling others with generosity (so people would like them) but not understanding that it is possible to harm others by giving them gifts with wrong motives. Before their Christian conversion this person would often feel weighted down in self-pity and depression, concerned about how people should be treating them.

After accepting Christ they discover the wonderful peace and joy derived from being generous and giving with a compassionate heart, having a genuine love and desire to help someone in need. They discover that being compassionate is a primary way to show their love for God. Then as they grow this person becomes more caring about other people while becoming less worried about their own circumstances

Personality Preference Fourth Pair

The MB forth pair is...
Judging / Perceiving
(Lifestyle)

The GQ new titles for these two preferences are...
Discerning / Long-Suffering
(Social)

This pair of personality preferences plays a major role in our decision-making, representing the social aspects of our life. These preferences function very closely in partnership with the 3rd pair in our decision-making, which represents the spiritual part of our life. MB with regards to these two preferences asks the following two questions.

In dealing with the outside world, do you prefer to get things decided or do you prefer to stay open to new information and options?

Do you prefer a more structured and decided lifestyle (Judging) or a more flexible and adaptable lifestyle (Perceiving)?

<u>Judging vs Discerning</u>
MB   GQ

The MB Judging person prefers a planned or orderly way of life, likes to have things settled and organized, feels more comfortable when decisions are made, and likes to bring life under control as much as possible. MB notes to not confuse the defined term Judging with judgmental, as they are not the same.

Describing how Christ followers change that have been Judging personalities in their past but once they become faithful believers transition into a GQ Discerning type personality may look like the following.

GQ Discerning

This person tends to prefer an orderly way of life. They like to organize and make decisions based on a plan that has been carefully thought out and under their control. They do allow themselves to be more spontaneous and long-suffering on some occasions but they generally plan for a certain amount or level of flexibility when planning and thinking about the future. Plans give them a sense of reality and stability, as they are typically uncomfortable without having any plans.

<u>Before & After their Christian transformation experience</u>

Before accepting Christ this Judging personality wanted to be in control of almost any given situation. They would rather make a bad decision than to sit and hope for the best by living with another person's choices. They never realized before having a relationship with Christ that God is in control. This personality, with maturity comes to realize that they don't really have control of every situation in their life.

After their conversion this person may still desire to be on a plan or schedule but they attempt to first validate if their plans are Godly and morally acceptable. This person begins either physically or mentally to develop a checklist (Discerning) of items they know are morally and biblically correct, while at the same time they learn that certain decisions are not in line with God's Word and should be banned from their list of choices. If it is against the principles of God, this person should decide to avoid making that choice.

<u>Perceiving vs Long-Suffering</u>

MB   GQ

The MB Perceiving person seems to prefer a flexible and spontaneous way of life and likes to understand and adapt to the world rather than organize it. Others often see this personality type as open to new experiences and information.

Describing how Christ followers change that have been Perceiving personalities once they become faithful believers into a GQ Long-Suffering type personality may look like the following.

GQ Long-Suffering

This personality enjoys spontaneity in life and being flexible and adaptable. The unknown and the excitement of discovery motivates their decision-making. The Long-Suffering find that sometimes they should have been more discerning as they become too comfortable going along with the flow and trusting that everything will be fine but sometimes this leaves them in troubling circumstances.

Before & After this person's Christian transformation experience

Before their Christian conversion there was a lot of confusion in this person's life. They could be influenced by many of the latest fads, concepts, and ideas. They find that most people liked them if they went along with their ideas and decisions but these type of choices would often be motivated by a desire to be popular and recognized. Some of these personality types actually believe that what ever anyone believes is OK and acceptable.

After finding Christ this person discovers that there are some absolute truths and that not every choice or behavior is acceptable. This personality may still enjoy being unstructured and learn that after they received Christ they should establish limits and boundaries on what they get involved with and how they handle relationships.

Discerning and Long-Suffering

Both the Discerning and Long-Suffering persons can be in the perfect Will of God and be living life according to the purpose and intention of God. God created people to be different and it is delightful to recognize the beauty and wonder of God's creation within each person. Often people that have been discerning their entire life can become more unstructured and spontaneous as they start to recognize and witness God's plan in action. They become more Long-Suffering and can enjoy a less structured lifestyle if and when they realize God is in control of all situations. Also the Long-Suffering person may learn to become more Discerning as they witness God has some specific rules and absolutes.

Both the Long-Suffering and Discerning persons can start to become aware of how the puzzle fits together in God's master plan for the good and perfect Will of God. The Discerning begin to see the sparkling of a snow flake and the Long-Suffering people start to realize that God does place discerning people in positions to calculate or analyze answers to issues that all result in the bringing about of God's wonderful plan. Both can realize that they can be fully satisfied and that God can satisfy their hunger and quench their thirst for Godly things. Both start to realize that marriages can really work, that children and parents can have wonderful relationships even when each person is a uniquely different creation of God and that we can be at peace even with those that have different personalities.

You can read more about how we develop and mature and what has the most influence on our life choices in my book titled, *My Bright Shining Star*. This book describes the various ways that we understand different important concepts and the four most important ingredients needed by all humans, which include acceptance, connection, respect, and love. In this book I also explain the critical role of heroes and mentors especially during the early years of childhood and adolescence.

Chemo Treatment Finally Finished

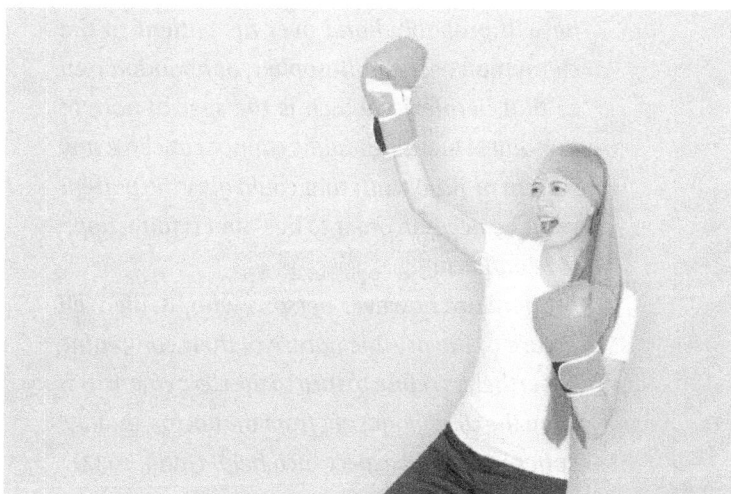

L ater in professor Carl Jung's life he made the following statement.

During the past thirty years, people from all the civilized countries of the earth have consulted me. I have treated many hundreds of patients...Among all my patients in the second half of life – that is to say, over thirty-five – there has not been one whose problem in the last resort was not that of finding a religious outlook on life...

> *It seems to me, that, side by side with the decline of religious life, the neuroses grow no-ticeable more frequent...*
>
> *The patient is looking for something that will take possession of him and give meaning and form to the confusion of his neurotic mind. Is the doctor equal to the task? To begin with, he will probably hand over his patient to the clergyman or the philosopher, or abandon him to that perplexity which is the special note of our day...Human thought cannot conceive any system or final truth that could give the patient what he needs in order to live: that is faith, hope, love and insight...*
>
> *There are however persons who, while well aware of the psychic nature of their complaint, nevertheless refuse to turn to the clergyman...It is from the clergyman, not from the doctor, that the sufferers should expect such help. (Jung, 1933)*

Missing the Mark

It is remarkable to me that such a brilliant man like Professor Jung could identify those four aspects of personality that so closely relate to the reality of the biblical truth of the Tetrahedron, yet he missed the mark. As did the other personality profiling examples of ancient times, which also came so close to identifying the four separate parts of humanity, yet they too missed the mark.

So I ask yet another question as I turned to the Bible once more,

> *Why have such brilliant educated people missed this important message of scripture?*

Luke chapter ten verse twenty-one is where I found one answer to my question.

> *At that time Jesus, full of joy through the Holy Spirit, said, "I praise you, Father, Lord of heaven and earth, because you have hidden these things from the wise and learned, and revealed them to little children. Yes, Father, for this is what you were pleased to do." (Luke 10:21 New International Version)*

Jung even came so very close to identifying humanity's needs for God but again lost the point when he referenced the clergyman or philosopher. The clergyman only points the way to the Great Physician, and the way to the great Healer. There is no one that can truly heal mankind or understand humanity except the Creator God. The clergyman can understand people's needs, and counsel them with good advice but only God truly understands our purpose. No one can be completely whole, satisfied, content, and happy unless they can find and follow God's designed purpose for their lives.

Trip Out West After Chemo and Radiation

R eflecting back on these new Bible secrets, I realized that most of the world wouldn't understand or accept this revelation given to me from God. My new revelation and inspiration would begin to drastically change how I observed the people around me and change how they perceived me. As I left my old viewpoints and perspective behind, I believed that my new outlook might start to isolate me from many as they would sense a change in my behavior and reactions. Discovering the unique personalities of each person when in my youth would often cause me to react in a negative or self-defensive critical fashion, but as I matured my judgment of people changed.

The environment I grew up in lacked diversity so it was common to judge people by their national origin, race, and culture, so misjudgment or misconceptions about others was common. People that displayed different customs in their lifestyles were labeled, shunned, and made fun of. Finally having opportunities in my life to experience friendships and work relationships with people from different cultures and different social / economic situations began to wash away my preconceived ideas.

I developed many close friendships with people who revealed my own cultural peculiarities and this made their differences more understandable and acceptable. When I was growing up I believed that my own family was the only normal family. Many years later I started saying my family is completely normal because they have just as many dysfunctions as everyone else's family. Over many years I started to understand that language, accent, and dialect can be ignored if true friendship exists in a relationship. We can learn and adjust our behavior and learn to appreciate the unique God created qualities of each person. We can discover that each personality was created for a very specific task and purpose in God's master plan.

Developing a Sunday school curriculum for a parenting class a few years ago, I took a closer look at each of the four GQ functions to see how the separate personality characteristics relate to each other. Exaggerating and placing each one of the four GQ groups out of proportion with the other three elements revealed some interesting personality traits.

Comparison

Those people that place their highest priority on the physical aspects of life will likely devalue the other three personality characteristics or place them in a lower position of significance. Physical gratification, self-satisfaction, indulgence, and self-realization are sought as the route to fulfillment. This Body-Man may use the other GQ personality aspects of the Mental, Social, and Spiritual as tools to achieve their physical objectives.

This personality may view people that live unhealthy physical lives as unintelligent and possibly less valuable to society. Placing the mind in the position of pleasure receptor, hoping to find mental stimulation from physical activities. The social relational becomes an avenue that leads to sensual pleasure or only to achieve procreation, like a species attempting to avoid extinction. Physical strength allows this personality to become self-centered or possibly turn into intimidators, willing to reach their objectives through physical domination.

The Mind-man which has placed priority on the academics is the next of the four groups. This person lives in a world of facts and figures, information and data. Believing that if enough academic knowledge can be obtained, enough data is collected, any of life's problems or issues can be resolved by the intellect of mankind. Humanistic is the name of their philosophy, believing that mankind can resolve all of the world issues with logic. An artificial reality which establishes a set of rules and regulations by which they normalize their decisions. This is a big bang theory of concepts, which is unable to be proven by scientific rational judgment, attempting to manipulate known facts which are based on assumptions that are mathematically impossible.

Placing emphasis on the mental aspects of life while devaluing the social and spiritual. Deemphasizing the physical but at the same time using the mind to achieve physical gratification. Using manipulative resourcing and sophisticated scheming, which are thought to be indicators of high intelligence. Forming small groups of devoted allies to empower their small kingdoms of influence, placing a low priority on social and spiritual issues brings about unstable relationships, and breeding conspiratorial apprehension and mistrust. Ignoring the spiritual aspects of life has violated the fundamental way that God created humans to be relational. Soon the Mental Man finds loneliness in isolation, which brings fear, depression, and paranoia.

The third group is the Socialite trendsetter, adjusting life decisions to correlate with events based largely on emotions and popularity. The extreme of this person's life looks for an abundance of recognition publicly or privately. Popularity is a key factor in the decision making of this type of person, which artificially stimulates their unrecognized spiritual nature. This social person often sways toward the type of personality that wants and desires to please everyone or on the negative side they understand people enough to be controlling and manipulative.

Finally the overly fanatical Spiritual Zealot thinks of themselves as so godly they are isolationist and antisocial. Life is spent attempting to follow rules and regulations believing they can achieve a perfect life through self-discipline and depredation. They often develop their own sects of religious activism headed in a direction of a destructive extremist.

Each of these exaggerated versions of the separated four personal characteristics can be witnessed to some degree in many people we know and associate with. So the real question that I ask myself was,

How does God use each of our individual strength and weaknesses to bring about our personal LIFE PLAN & PURPOSE?

I also questioned,

How do we balance and prioritize each of our four personality characteristics?

Watching a Beautiful Sunrise in Utah

Taking a look at each of the three God Quad elements while also illuminating the Spiritual reveals some noteworthy personality characteristics. In each examination I determined that when people ignore or deny the Spiritual, one of the other three GQ features is elevated to the position of Decision Maker.

The Body-Man is a wild, vicious beast that roams the earth

to devour all that can be obtained, as they overpower the weak and meek. Training their offspring to overcome their enemies with violence and taking what they can find. Sensual pleasure, addictions, satisfaction of all the senses becomes the primary choice of life decisions.Without acknowledgment of a life beyond, sex and procreation are the only human link to eternity, hoping to achieve a connection to the future.

The Mind-Man replaces the spiritual with cognitive mental logic, writing many laws, rules and regulations in a vain attempt to control cultural behavior; placing leadership in the hands of the intellectual educated but finds that there is discord among the tribal leaders; lacking any type of ethics the mind can become a weapon of mass destruction, and a tool to manipulate, control, and destroy. The mind of a highly intelligent person with a bright intellect can make a choice to use their knowledge for evil, selfish purpose or attempts to save the world with logic.

Now the Socialite will aspire to great popularity with good deeds and charity, while they substitute the Social for the Spiritual by becoming the champion of a cause. Loving to be in the spotlight at one end of the spectrum or finding a deep sense of personal satisfaction knowing how to use social interactions to manage or manipulate their relationships with others. The socialite can become a great actor, deceiving even those closest friends and family. A true chameleon, able to change and adapt to almost any situation as they understand interpersonal complex relationships and creatively use people's personalities to manipulate and get what they want. But deep-seated conflict and hatred rules the heart of this person because they can never reveal their true identity. Imagine a truly physically talented, mentally gifted, socially brilliant person without any truly close relationships, which will become a very unhappy person. As Anican Skywalker in the Star War series started as a child prodigy and later turned to the dark side to become Darth Vader(LucasFilm Ltd., 2013).

A Hotel Overlooking the Virgin River Valley

I believe that psychologists Jung, Alder, and Freud had a primary failure in their thinking and that was to ignore and account for the most dynamic ingredient in personality, which is the Spiritual.

This raised yet another question in my mind,

What does the Spiritual look like in the unsaved unbeliev-ing person?

Or...

Can a person live without or ignore this spiritual aspect of personality?

Let me quote something from another book by M. Robert Mulholland Jr. titled, *Invitation to a Journey* where I found my answer to this question.

Before we allowed Jesus to exercise any degree of lordship, we were the lord of our lives...our will, our desire, our interest, our agenda, our program, our plan, our purpose, our wants, our needs regulated our existence. We were in control of our own being, and under our own control we developed a whole structure of habits, attitudes, perspectives, dynamics of relationship, ways of reacting and responding to the world around us. We developed, you might say, a body of being made up of this complex network of habits and attitudes. The entire network was constructed under our own lordship. (Mulholland, 1993)

A majority of the current culture of the world we live in attempts to live life in this manner. The concept of keeping God out of school and government is an obvious objective in today's society. Without the Spiritual aspect in a person's life the other three elements of Physical, Social, and Mental become unbalanced and out of proportion.

That special God-created element that cannot be quenched as

in thirst, that secret seed planted within our life that mankind may sense for a lifetime but may sadly never discover. In our humanity we so easily deny, ignore, run away from, incorrectly name and identify, and cover up as well as attempt to re-define the spiritual. Many discover that it cannot be ignored for it is God created, God designed, God planted, and cannot simply be discarded or thrown away. As I grow older and look into the mirror I see my dad's likeness more and more each day, whether I like it or not, so like our DNA we cannot deny our spiritual nature.

This is one reason people position one of the other three elements of the God Quad as their primary controller. Others may combine all three elements, excluding the spiritual and consider this,

...who they are.

Mulholland called this their, Body of Being. This *who they are* sounds a lot like the Heart and Soul, or Heart that I described earlier, but it is a cheap, incomplete copy or imitation of the real Heart and Soul of mankind that God created.

People may also place objects or possessions in the place of the Spiritual. Money and wealth, popularity, sex, or maybe career, hobbies, and relationships and family can be elevated to the position and level of the Spiritual. Satan is a liar and he convinces people, confuses people, and manipulates people into believing they are the LORD of their own life.

When people leave the Spiritual out of their life people develop a Humanistic viewpoint and perspective of life. People with a humanistic view of life develop a tendency to have no absolutes which brings about an internalized evolving world that is constantly changing, being redesigned, and rethought. The humanistic lifestyle becomes ever more increasingly internalized and self-focused, self centered, and less outwardly focused. Arrogance and conceit are likely to occur, which deteriorates relationships, causing conflict and isolation.

Testimony of My Travels on a Treasure Hunt

I believe it would have been much better if my wife could have avoided getting cancer, but treatment was better than the alternative. Prevention is preferred over treatment, but to properly treat my wife's cancer the doctors first had to properly diagnose her sickness. If God and the Spiritual element have been eliminated, ignored, or dismissed it will always cause irregularities, peculiarities, and imbalance in a person's life. These abnormalities will never have a correct antidote or cure if we don't first detect and identify how humans are created.

As noted earlier I once tore out an electrical regulator from an old boat using the worthless manual I purchased to make the repairs. The boat motor manual was unusable but I also forgot to trace all of the wires and label them. Then after purchasing the replacement part, it had a different appearance and the wiring connections were different than the old ones. It took me many hours even after reading the manual to figure out just where all the wires should go. I was lucky that some of the misconnected wires during my trial and error didn't blow something up.

When mankind attempts to DO LIFE without God, wires get misconnected and life does not work the way God designed it to function. God uses each personality type and the uniqueness of each person to play a part in his Master Plan. The complexities of personality, friendships, and relations, along with every factor in our life play an important part in God's perfect blueprint for our lives. It becomes clear that no person can understand the complexities of our life in combination with every other person's life and events. God is the ONLY one that has the authority, intelligence, strength, knowledge, and wisdom to be in control.

Prevention is a method by which we correctly identify how we were created, who created us, and understand that only God has the ability and wisdom to guide and direct us toward maturity. We must start this prevention of problems by including the key factor in a well-balanced, mature life that is found in the Spiritual element of life.

Come join me on this journey, on a search for the many

wonderful treasures of God found hidden in the Big Black Book. God is an awesome, powerful, amazing, loving, wise, creator, friend, defender, and father. He leads me when I'm willing, he speaks to me when I listen, and he is willing to guide me when I'll follow. An adventure lesson in maturity and a relationship instruction that has truly inspired my thinking and living.

The Healthy Life After Treatment

I nstead of being motivated by selfish physical desire and ambitions it is far better to transition toward unselfish sharing. Changing from living a life of mere existence to one of designed creative purpose.

Moving from calculative into imaginative, from manipulative to relational. Transitioning from an inward selfishness to an outward focus toward others.

Transitioning from a small restrictive world into an unlimited universe to be discovered. Living a life not limited and restricted but a life of unlimited total freedom.

Being transformed from ruled by nature to being ruled by an abiding Spirit.

Making a conversion from living with a desire to achieve Power and Control but in its place allowing the almighty God of the universe to work his power in and through me.

Maturing in my Need to Adapt, to a desire to belong as I learn to become respected accepted and loved.

Finally discovering my true Heart and Soul or Heart, moving beyond my Body of Being and who I am. Living life with my mind set on the Spirit instead of on my old selfish nature.

Learning to live the unnatural instead of the natural and becoming more Godlier and less Humanistic.

I am trying more each day to move from selfish, greedy, lustful, lonesomeness, into loving, sharing, and joyful companionship with others. From a place of fear, disgrace, embarrassment, and hatred to a place of peace, acceptance, and belonging. From a place of aimless wondering, lostness, confusion and distrust to a place of clear direction, guidance, clarity, and trust. From spiritual poverty, emptiness and being cursed to Spiritual wealth, fulfillment and a life of blessings.

This is a gradual process that requires trust and obedience. Often failing but hopefully learning from my mistakes and asking God to forgive me when I fail and having God guide me on my corrective pathway.

God, I need your treatment for my ailments, your patience with my anxiousness, your mentoring for my immaturity, and your love for my deep need of acceptance.

Pretty Much Back to Normal Life

Now I am being guided down a pathway, following a new treasure map, which sparkles like a magical land of delights. Revealing many new questions I need to ask and finding new answers, other mysteries to unravel. This journal has been fun and exciting to write but only a small part of my search for the God of all Creation. The God Quad is an answer to only a few of my many questions.

The Tetrahedron revealed the story of my personal adventure leading me to my next question, which is to determine how a family should function and why we make the choices that we make. I'll begin my new search by asking why God so highly values relationships and family. The answers must be able to be found in this same big black book if family is such a high priority to God. The parables and stories, the life pattern of Christ and other Bible heroes must have set an example of what God wants me to discover.

Now Lord, I want to thank you for helping my wife and me through our struggles over the last few years dealing with this cancer. I will continue to praise and worship you as I continue along my trail of lifetime adventures on my search for your hidden treasures.

Dennis E. Stamm

My counsel is this: Live freely, animated and motivated by God's Spirit. Then you won't feed the compulsions of selfishness. For there is a root of sinful self-interest in us that is at odds with a free spirit, just as the free spirit is incompatible with selfishness. These two ways of life are antithetical, so that you cannot live at times one way and at times another way according to how you feel on any given day. Why don't you choose to be led by the Spirit and so escape the erratic compulsions of a law-dominated existence? (Galatians 5: 16-18 The Message Bible)

References

Adler, A. (1964). The Individual Psychology of Alfred Adler. H. L. Ansbacher and R. R. Ansbacker (Eds.). New York: Harper Torchbooks.

Bridges, J. (1978). The Pursuit of Holiness. Colorado Springs: NavPress.

Briggs, K. C. (1987). Myers Briggs Type Indicator. Form G. Palo Alto, Calif: Consulting Psychologists Press.

Freud S. (1923) The Ego and the Id. The Standard Edition of the Complete Psychological Works of Sigmund Freud, Volume XIX.

Jung, C. G. (1921). Psychological Types. The Collected Works of C. G. Jung, Vol. 6, Bollingen Series XX.

Jung, C. G. (1933) Modern Man in Search of a Soul. New York: Harcourt, Brace & World.

Jung C. G. (1971). 'General Description of the Types', in Psychological Types, Collected Works vol. 6, Ch. X. London: Routledge and Kegan Paul.

LucasFilm Ltd,; 20th Century Fox (2013). Star Wars Original Trilogy. [San Francisco]: Beverly Hills, California; Lucasfilm; Twentieth Century Fox Home Entertainment.

Mulholland, M. R. (1993). Invitation to a Journey: A Road Map for Spiritual Formation. Downers Grove, IL: Intervarsity Press.

Image Credits

A Trip on a Big Pink Plane

Airplane and Clouds
Original AI generated by hired illustrator using perchance.org

Chicken
freepik.com
Free usage – attributed to creator: juliaizhuk

A Few Nights in a Hotel By Mickey Mouse

Mickey Mouse
commons.wikimedia.com
Public Domain Image

Abraham Lincoln
commons.wikimedia.com
Public Domain Image

While my Wife was Shopping for Orchids

Orchids
  Original AI generated by hired illustrator using perchance.org

One Last Night by Mickey's Place

Castle
  Original AI generated by hired illustrator using perchance.org

Sitting in My Wife's Doctor's Office

Medical Bag and Stethoscope
  Original AI generated by hired illustrator using perchance.org

The First Day in Surgery

Hospital
  commons.wikimedia.com
  Public Domain Image

Starting the First Day of Chemo

Abraham Lincoln
  commons.wikimedia.com
  Public Domain Image

Ribbon
  pexels.com
  Free usage - attributed to author: Tara Winstead

Bible on Table with Candle
  Original AI generated by hired illustrator using perchance.org

Student in Thought
  Original AI generated by hired illustrator using perchance.org

Another Day in Chemo

Inspiration
  dreamstime.com
  Free usage - author credit ID3115362427

One Wednesday Evening After Church

Praying
  freepik.com
  Free image

Home Alone When My Wife is in the Hospital

Bridge Over River Valley
  needpix.com
  Free image

Despair
  Original AI generated by hired illustrator using perchance.org

Couple
  freepik.com
  Free image - Author credit AI generated by almesran5009

Home with My Wife After a Hospital Stay

The Four Suits
  commons.wikimedia.com
  Public Domain Image

Back to Finish Up Chemo

Christ Teaching
  commons.wikimedia.com
  Public Domain Image

Back in the Hospital

Child on Rock
  Google Creative Commons
  Free Image - Author credit: Eli's Art Pad, Eli Moody

Nearly Complete with Chemo

Cross and Dove
   Clipart-library.com
   Free Usage

Wife at Home in Recovery

Recovering Woman
   illust.com clipart
   Free Usage

Four-Leaf Clover
   Pixby.com
   Free Usage

A Memory of Past Events

Silhouette of Woman on a Tree Swing
   Clipart – stock.adobe.com
   Free Usage

Christ Teaching Disciples
   Google Creative Commons
   Free Image – Author Credit: jgcv46

One Inspired Evening as My Wife was Recovering

Inspiration
 Clipart – istockphoto.com
 Free Image

God Quad
 AI Generated Google Gemini
 Copyright Dennis Stamm (owned by the author)

A Time of Reflection on a Cruise Ship

Reflection
 clipartpanda.com clipart
 Free Image (watermark unidentifiable through research)

God Quad
 AI Generated Google Gemini
 Copyright Dennis Stamm (owned by the author)

Chemo Treatments Finally Finished

Beating Cancer
 dreamstime.com
 Free Image

Puzzle
 depositphotos.com clipart
 Free Image – Author Credit: ronieishman ID#14002503

Trip Out West After Chemo and Radiation

Dude Ranch
  everypixel.com
  Free Image

Watching a Beautiful Sunrise in Utah

Utah Sunrise
  commons.wikimedia.com
  Public Domain Image

A Hotel Overlooking the Virgin River Valley

River Valley
  commons.wikimedia.com
  Public Domain Image

Testimony of My Travels on a Treasure Hunt

Treasure Box
  commons.wikimedia.com
  Free Image

A Healthy Life After Treatment

Mother Teresa
  commons.wikimedia.org
  Public Domain Image

About the Author

Teaching children and teenagers has been a lifetime joy for me over the last 50 years. Using my architecture and construction experience to help churches and Christian schools has been a real blessing as I raised my own three children. After retiring, I now enjoy grand parenting as I continue to teach part time at a Christian school and writing.

Also by Dennis Stamm

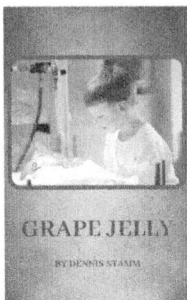

Grape Jelly

A must have for all new parents that want to raise truly successful children. A practical common sense book about parenting that is written in a way that makes parenting more easy to understand. Methods and techniques that teach, train, and develop children into mature, responsible adults. How to modify behavior and lead children to a bright future.

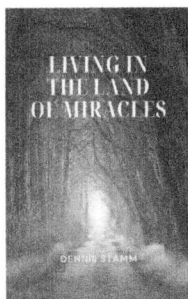

Living in the Land of Miracles

Finding a Magical Land of Enchantment. Discovering a pathway through life that leads to the Creator. Find this hidden path using hints, secrets, and treasures of God, leading to an Everlasting Place.

My Bright Shining Star

Help your child and teen through the different stages of life: Dependence, Independence, Interdependence, Leading to God, and Redemption. Mentors, heroes, teachers, and family have a heavy influence on our choices and decisions. Finding our way to a brighter future as we walk along this pathway of life.

Made in the USA
Monee, IL
09 December 2024

71233876R00075